JUMPIN' JIM'S™ '60s UKE-IN

Compiled and Arranged by Jim Beloff

Edited by Ronny S. Schiff
Cover and Art Direction by Elizabeth Maihock Beloff
Graphics and Music Typography by Charylu Roberts

FOREWORD

On the fun scale of one to ten, this book was an eleven. First of all, as someone who came of musical age in the 1960s, this was a chance to play with songs that I related to i a very personal way. Virtually all of these songs are tied somehow to my earliest memories of popular music, whether hearing it on the radio, using my allowance to buy it, dancing to it or using it as the soundtrack to my typically turbulent teenage life.

Secondly, it was a fascinating experiment to see if songs that were primarily of the rock 'n' roll era could work on a ukulele. In particular, it was very interesting to learn what songs worked especially well. For example, John Sebastian's Lovin' Spoonful songs seemed to be tailor-made for strumming as did the shuffle beat songs of Burt Bacharach. Even songs like "Girl From Ipanema" with its beautiful jazz chords seemed to thrive on the uke. Most notable was just how well so many of the Beatles songs sounded. As I played through their catalogue, I would gasp at the beauty of many of the chord change proving yet again the enduring quality of their songwriting. Of course, I had to include "Tip-Toe Thru' The Tulips With Me." This song wasn't written in the '60s, but it was a bi hit in 1968 thanks to Tiny Tim.

Finally, it was a dream come true to find that a mutual love for the ukulele could bring about a meeting with George Harrison. His "appreciation" on the opposite page came about after an afternoon of strumming a wondrous stew of songs made famous by George Formby, Elvis, Otis Redding and Joni Mitchell, as well as new songs he had written on the uke. The afternoon also featured a uke version of his classic song "Something," which I'm very happy to include here.

Many thanks to Linda Arias, Wendy DeWitt, Danny Ferrington, Richard Green, George Harrison, Doug Haverty, Sam Neill, Charylu Roberts, Ronny Schiff, Tommy Steel Peter Thomas and, of course, Liz. It truly has been "Ukedelic!"

—*Jumpin' Jim*
Los Angeles, CA 1999

Also Available: (**Books**) *Jumpin' Jim's Ukulele Favorites; Jumpin' Jim's Ukulele Tips 'N' Tune Jumpin' Jim's Ukulele Gems, Jumpin' Jim's Ukulele Christmas; The Ukulele: A Visual History* (**CDs**) *Jim's Dog Has Fleas; For The Love Of Uke; Legends Of Ukulele* (**Video**) The Joy Of Uke

FLEA MARKET MUSIC, INC.
BOX 1127, STUDIO CITY, CALIFORNIA 91614

2/2/99.

Everybody should have and play a 'UKE' its so simple to carry with you and it is one instrument you cant play and not laugh! Its so sweet and also very old — some are made of wood — some are made of armadillo's. I love them — the more the MERRIER — EveRyone I know who is into the Ukulele is 'cRackeRs' so get yourself a few and enjoy yourselves — love from George (Keoki) ॐ HarRison

CHORD CHART

Tune Ukulele
G   C   E   A

MAJOR CHORDS

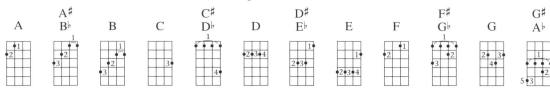

MINOR CHORDS

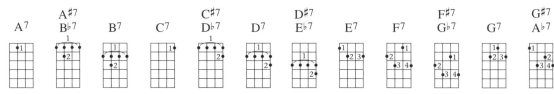

DOMINANT SEVENTH CHORDS

DOMINANT NINTH CHORDS

MINOR SEVENTH CHORDS

MAJOR SIXTH CHORDS

MINOR SIXTH CHORDS

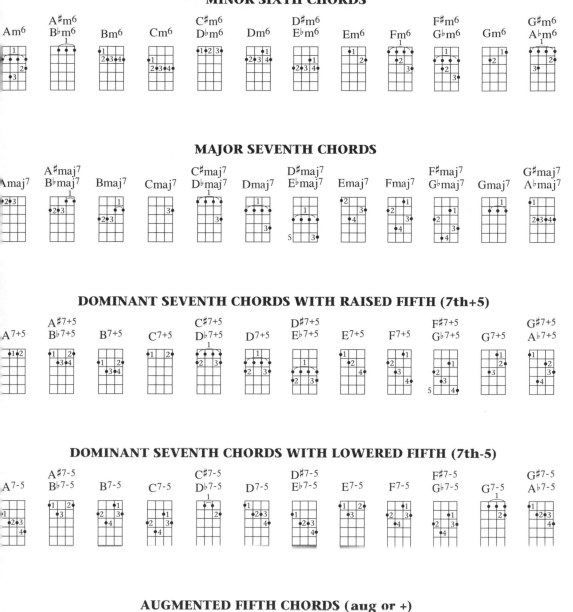

MAJOR SEVENTH CHORDS

DOMINANT SEVENTH CHORDS WITH RAISED FIFTH (7th+5)

DOMINANT SEVENTH CHORDS WITH LOWERED FIFTH (7th-5)

AUGMENTED FIFTH CHORDS (aug or +)

DIMINISHED SEVENTH CHORDS (dim)

ALL MY LOVING

Words and Music by
JOHN LENNON and PAUL McCARTNE

BUILD ME UP, BUTTERCUP

Words and Music by
TONY McCAULEY and MICHAEL D'ABO

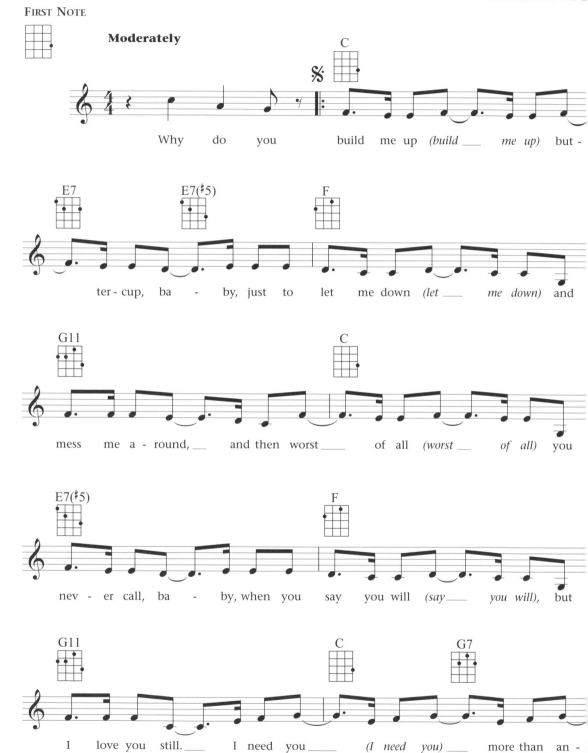

an - y more, ___ it's not you, _____ you let me
ed to you ___ all the more, _____ why do I

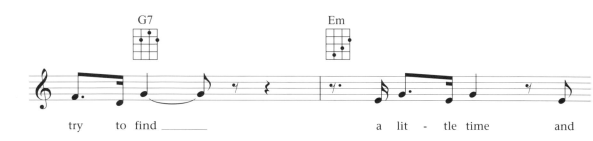

down a - gain. _____ Ba - by, ba - by, ___
need you so? _____

try to find _____ a lit - tle time and

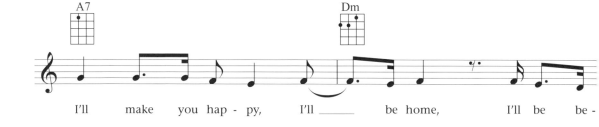

I'll make you hap - py, I'll _____ be home, I'll be be -

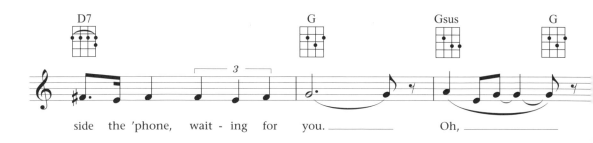

side the 'phone, wait - ing for you. _____ Oh, _____

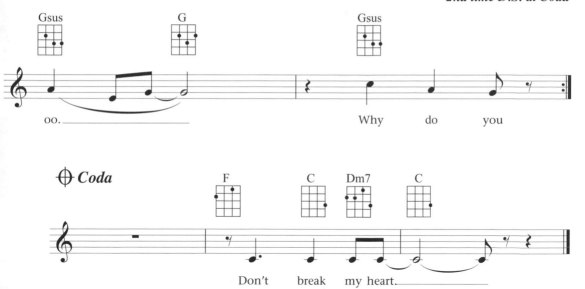

oo._____ Why do you

⊕ *Coda*

Don't break my heart._____

Tuning Your Uke

The smallest and most popular size of the ukulele is the soprano. All of the songs in this book were arranged for the soprano ukulele in C tuning. Nonetheless, if you tune any sized uke as shown below, you will be able to play the chords as written.

The easiest way to tune the ukulele is with a pitch pipe, matching the strings with the notes:

This corresponds to that famous melody:

Here are the notes on the keyboard:

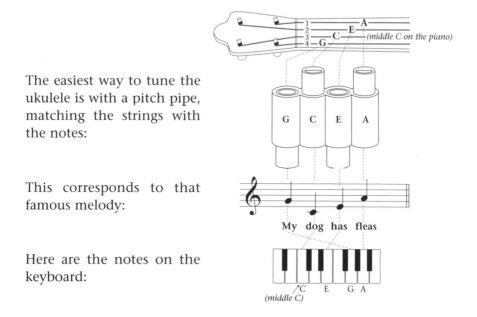

DAYDREAM

Words and Music by
JOHN SEBASTIAN

day - dream - in' boy. ___ And I'm lost in a day - dream, ___

dream - in' 'bout my bun - dle of joy. ___ *Whistles* _ _ _ _ _ _ _ _

Repeat and Fad

3. *Whistle*
   Whistle
   Whistle
   Whistle
   And you can be sure that if you're feelin' right,
   a daydream will last till long into the night.
   Tomorrow at breakfast you may pick up your ears,
   or you may be daydreamin' for a thousand years.

Have a nice day

(SITTIN' ON) THE DOCK OF THE BAY

Words and Music by
OTIS REDDING and STEPHEN CROPPER

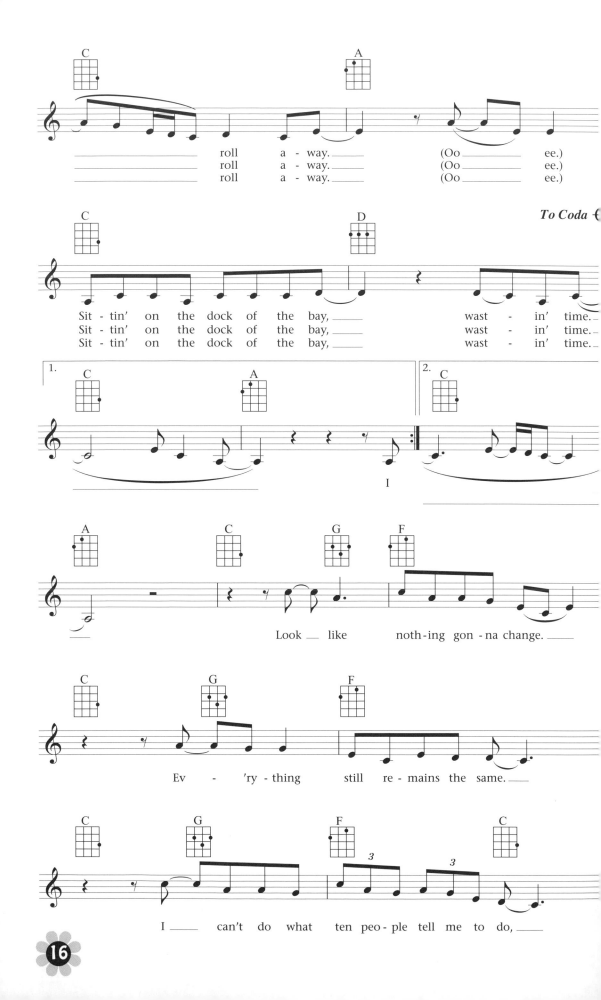

To Coda

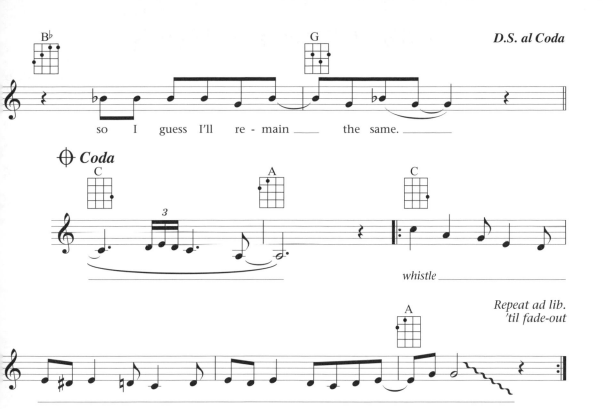

so   I   guess I'll   re - main ____ the   same. ____

whistle ____

*Repeat ad lib.
'til fade-out*

Transposing

When you want to change the key of a song (for instance if it's too high or low to sing), it is necessary to change all of the chords. In order to do this, it's just a matter of counting up or down the scale. Here's a chart that will make this easier to do:

Chords in		MAJOR			MINOR		
C:		C	F	G7	Am	Dm	E7
D♭:		D♭	G♭	A♭7	B♭m	E♭m	F7
D:		D	G	A7	Bm	Em	F♯7
E♭:		E♭	A♭	B♭7	Cm	Fm	G7
E:		E	A	B7	C♯m	F♯m	G♯7
F:		F	B♭	C7	Dm	Gm	A7
G♭:		G♭	C♭	D♭7	E♭m	A♭m	B♭7
G:		G	C	D7	Em	Am	B7
A♭:		A♭	D♭	E♭7	Fm	B♭m	C7
A:		A	D	E7	F♯m	Bm	C♯7
B♭:		B♭	E♭	F7	Gm	Cm	D7
B:		B	E	F♯7	G♯m	C♯m	D♯7

For example, if you wish to transpose a song in the key of C to the key of D, you would...

	The Original Chord		The New Chord
change	C	to	D
change	F	to	G
change	G7	to	A7
change	Am	to	Bm
change	Dm	to	Em
change	E7	to	F♯7

In this case, everything moves up one whole step.

DAYDREAM BELIEVER

Words and Music by
JOHN STEWART

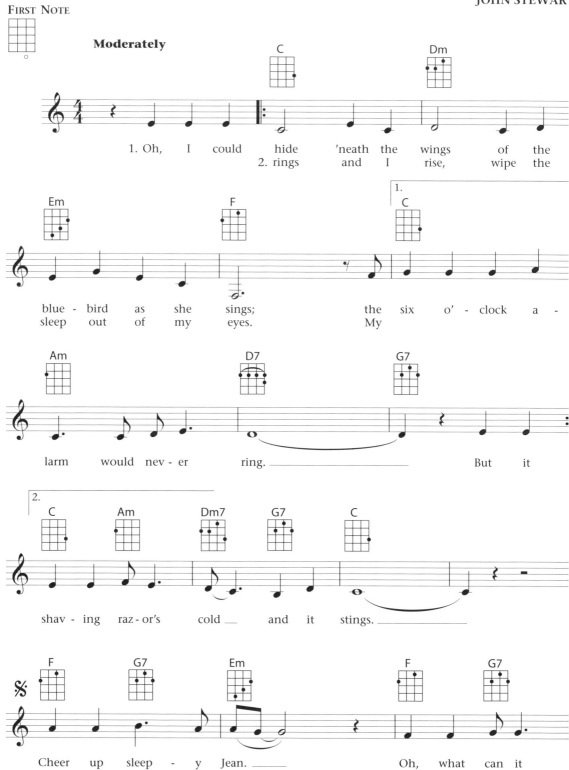

1. Oh, I could hide 'neath the wings of the blue-bird as she sings; the six o'-clock a-larm would nev-er ring. _____ But it

2. rings and I rise, wipe the sleep out of my eyes. My shav-ing raz-or's cold ___ and it stings. _____

Cheer up sleep-y Jean. _____ Oh, what can it

D.S. and fade

EIGHT DAYS A WEEK

Words and Music by
JOHN LENNON and PAUL McCARTNEY

show I care. __ { Ooh I need your love, babe, __ guess you know it's true __
Love you ev - 'ry day, girl, __ al - ways on my mind. __

__ Hope you need my love, babe, __ just like I need you. __
__ One thing I can say, girl, __ love you all the time. __

__ { Hold me, __ love me. __ Hold me, __ love me. __ I

ain't got noth - in' but love, babe, __ eight days a week, __

eight days a week, __ eight days a week. __

GEORGY GIRL

Words by
JIM DALE

Music by
TOM SPRINGFIELD

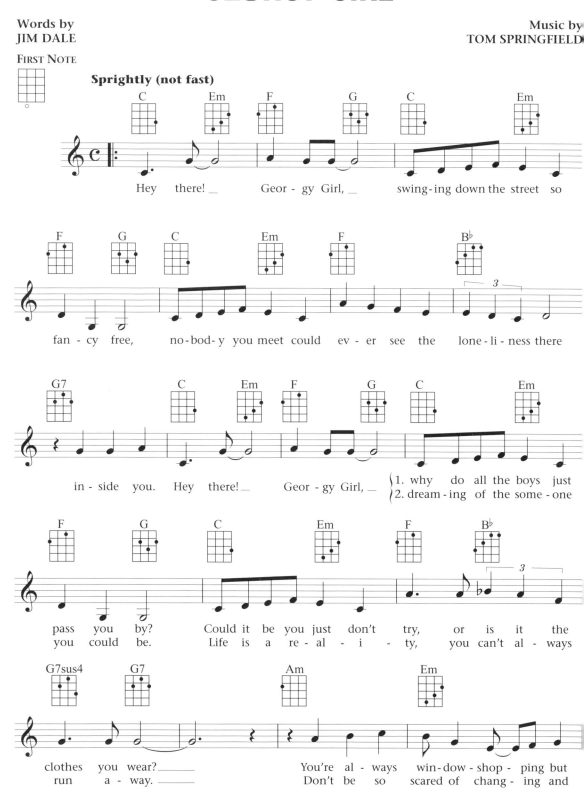

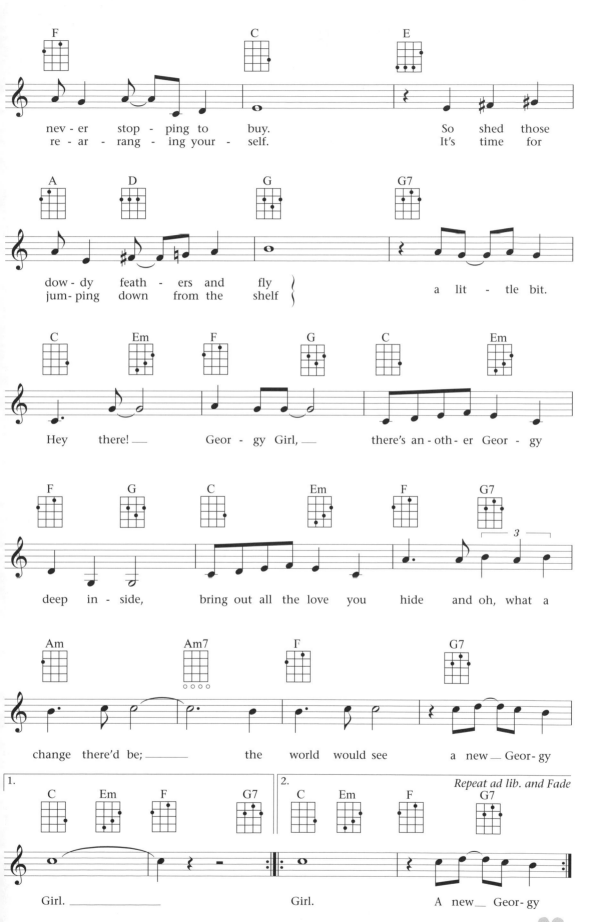

THE GIRL FROM IPANEMA

English Words by NORMAN GIMBEL
Original Words by VINICIUS DeMORAES

Music by
ANTONIO CARLOS JOBIM

24

she pass - es, each one ___ she } pass - es goes
he pass - es each girl ___ he }

"a-a-h!" ___   Oh, ___

___ but I watch { her } so sad - ly. ___
                  { him }

___   How ___   can I tell { her } I
                                              { him }

love { her? ___ }   Yes, ___
     { him? ___ }

___ I would give my heart glad - ly, ___

but each day when {she/he} walks to the sea, {she/he} looks straight a - head not at me. Tall and tan and young — and {love - ly, the girl ——/hand - some, the boy ——} from I - pa - ne - ma goes walk - ing, and when —— {she/he} pass - es I smile, —— but {she/he} does - n't see.

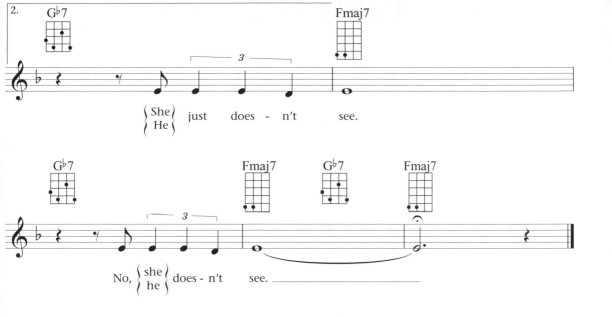

2.

G♭7   Fmaj7

{ She / He } just does - n't see.

G♭7   Fmaj7   G♭7   Fmaj7

No, { she / he } does - n't see. _____

Tall and tan and young and uking…(Courtesy of Capitol Records)

27

HAPPY TOGETHER

Words and Music by
GARRY BONNER and ALAN GORDON

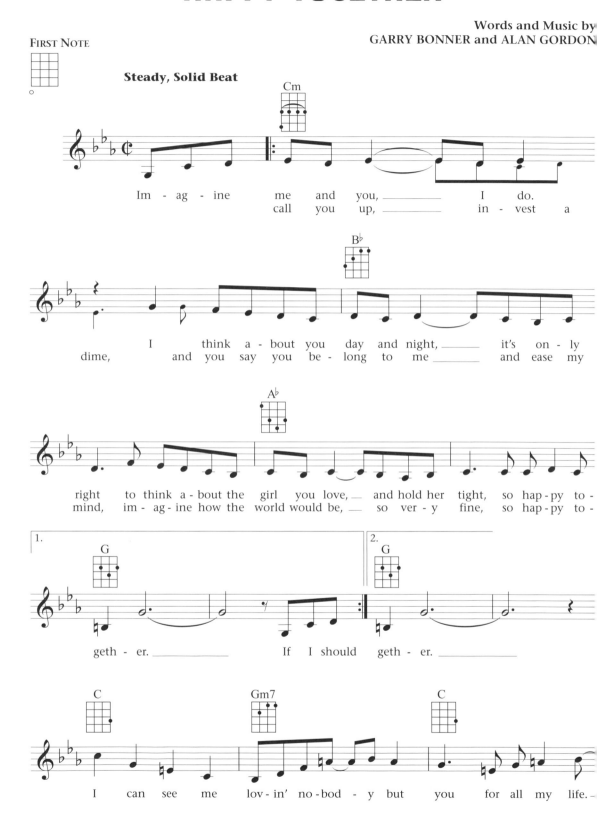

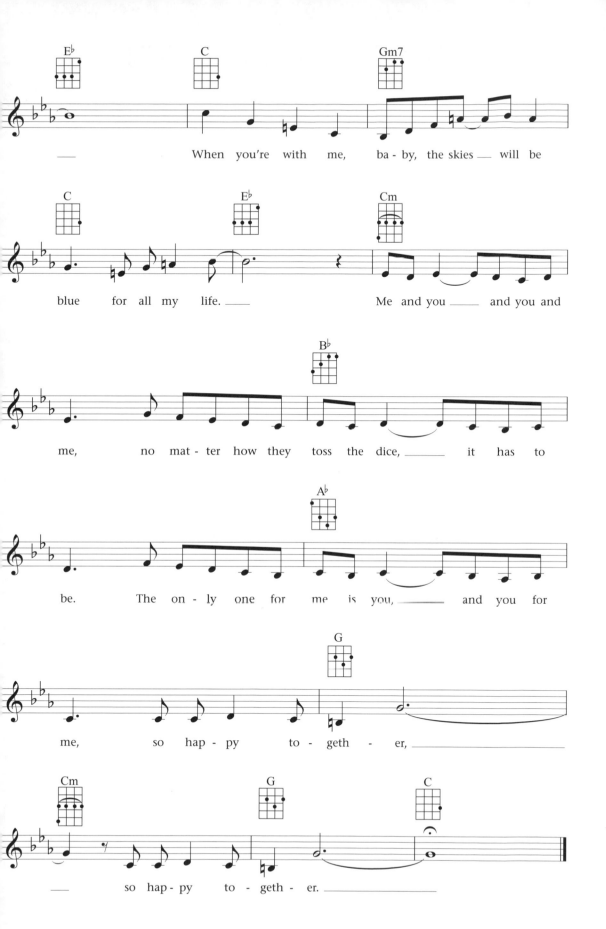

HERE COMES THE SUN

Words and Music by
GEORGE HARRISON

Lit - tle dar - ling, it's been __ a long, __ cold, lone - ly win-
Lit - tle dar - ling, the smiles __ re - turn - ing to __ their fac-
Lit - tle dar - ling, I feel __ that ice __ is slow - ly melt-

ter; lit - tle dar - ling, it feels __ like years __
es; lit - tle dar - ling, it seems __ like years __
ing; lit - tle dar - ling, it seems __ like years __

__ since it's been here. __
__ since it's been here. __
__ since it's been clear. __   Here comes __ the sun, __

here comes __ the sun, __ and I say "It's all __ right."

To Coda

1.

2.

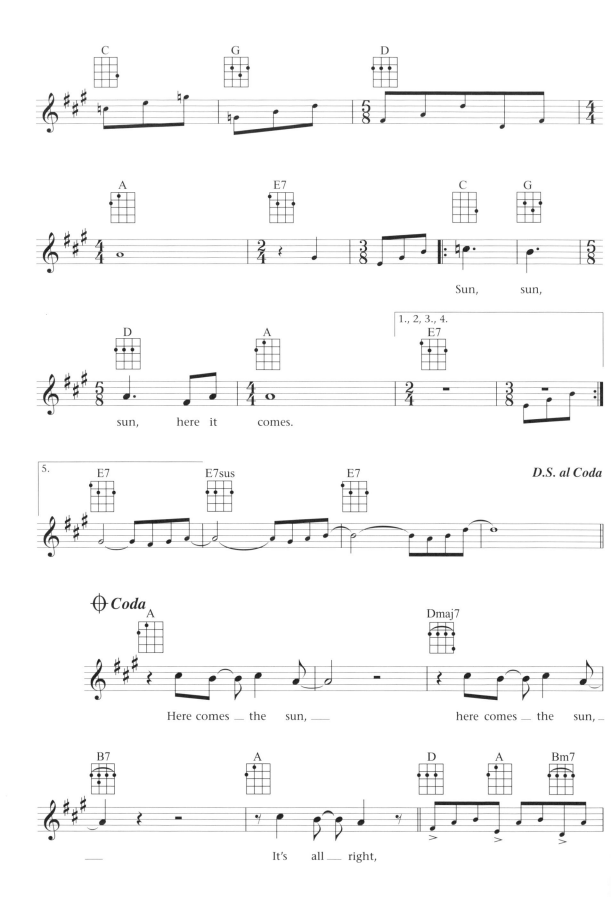

Sun, sun,

sun, here it comes.

D.S. al Coda

Here comes — the sun, — here comes — the sun, —

— It's all — right,

It's all — right.

Courtesy of NASA

Here comes the earth...

I WILL

Words and Music by
JOHN LENNON and PAUL McCARTNEY

KING OF THE ROAD

Words and Music by
ROGER MILLER

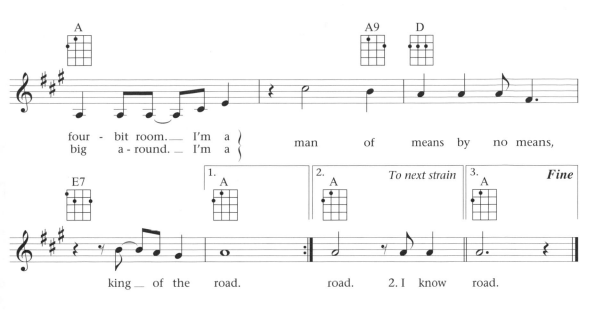

four - bit room.___ I'm a } big a - round. ___ I'm a } man of means by no means,

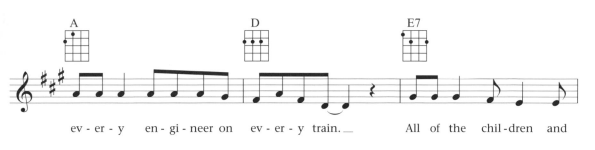

king ___ of the road. road. 2. I know road.

ev - er - y en - gi - neer on ev - er - y train. ___ All of the chil - dren and

all of their names, ___ and ev - er - y hand - out in ev - er - y town, ___ and

D.S. al Fine

ev - 'ry lock that ain't locked when no one's a - round. 3. I sing

MELLOW YELLOW

Words and Music by
DONOVAN LEITCH

FIRST NOTE

Moderately Slow, with a "Rock" Beat

1. I'm just mad a - bout Saf - fron, a -
2. I'm just mad a - bout Four - teen a -
3. Born high for - ev - er to fly, a -

Saf - fron's mad a - bout me. A -
Four - teen's mad a - bout me. A -
wind - a - ve - loc - i - ty nil.

I'm - a just mad a - bout Saf - fron,
I'm - a just mad a - bout Four - teen,
Born high for - ev - er to fly;

she's just mad a - bout me. } They call me Mel - low
she's just mad a - bout me. }
if you want your cup I will fill. }

Spoken: "Quite rightly"

Yel - low, they call me Mel - low

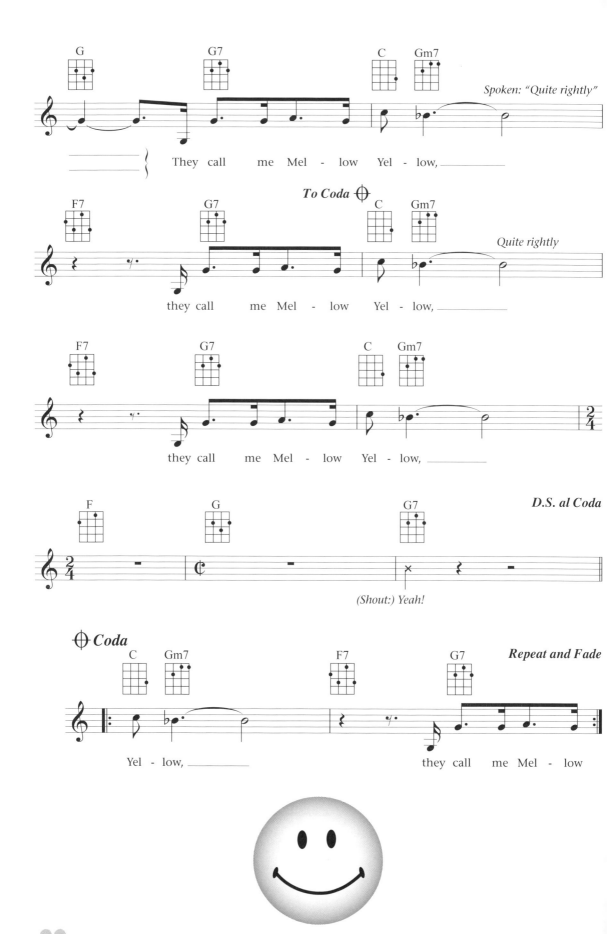

MICHELLE

Words and Music by
JOHN LENNON and PAUL McCARTNEY

41

MOON RIVER

Lyric by
JOHNNY MERCER

Music by
HENRY MANCINI

PENNY LANE

Words and Music by
JOHN LENNON and PAUL McCARTNEY

back.   And the bank - er nev - er wears a mac ___
trim.   And then the fire - man rush - es in ___

___ in the pour - ing rain,   ver - y strange! ___ Pen - ny Lane
    from the pour - ing rain,   ver - y strange! ___ Pen - ny Lane

___ is in my ears ___ and in my eyes, ___
___ is in my ears ___ and in my eyes, ___

wet be - neath the blue ___ sub - ur - ban skies ___
there be - neath the blue ___ sub - ur - ban skies ___

To Coda ⊕

___ I sit.   And mean - while back in Pen - ny Lane
___ I sit.

___ there is a fire - man with an hour - glass, ___ and in his pock -

et is a por - trait of the Queen. He likes to

keep his fire - en - gine clean; — It's a clean — ma - chine.

RAINDROPS KEEP FALLIN' ON MY HEAD

Lyric by
HAL DAVID

Music by
BURT BACHARACH

First Note

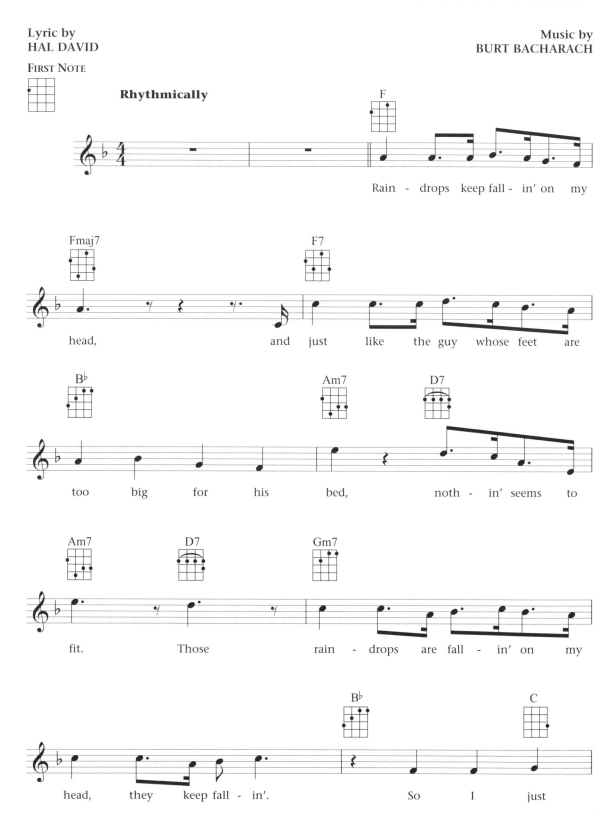

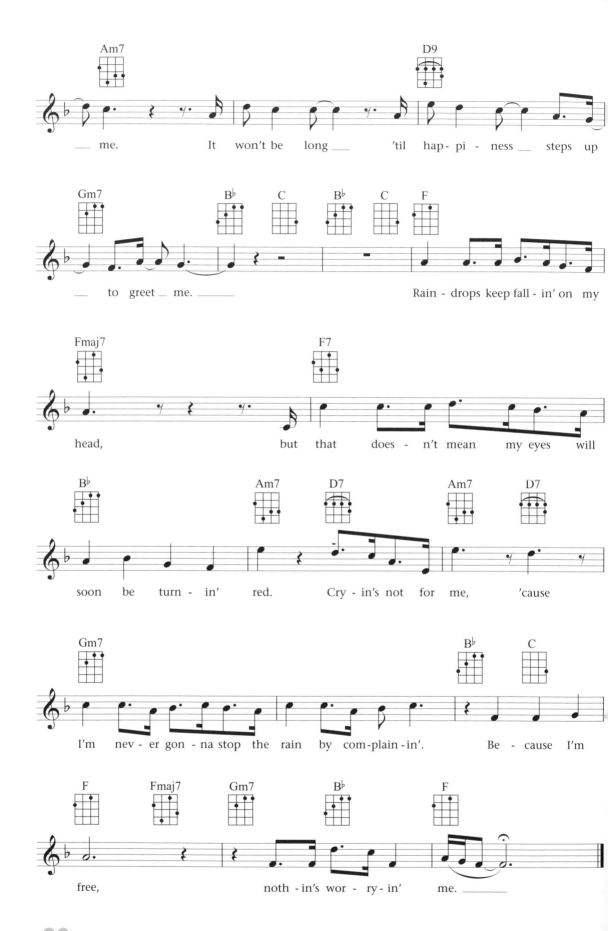

me. It won't be long ___ 'til hap-pi-ness ___ steps up

___ to greet ___ me. _____ Rain-drops keep fall-in' on my

head, but that does-n't mean my eyes will

soon be turn-in' red. Cry-in's not for me, 'cause

I'm nev-er gon-na stop the rain by com-plain-in'. Be-cause I'm

free, noth-in's wor-ry-in' me. _____

The Family Of Ukuleles

Because the most common ukulele size is the soprano (generally 21" in length), this book has been written for the soprano ukulele (or any ukulele tuned GCEA). Ukes, however, come in many sizes. The baritone ukulele (generally 31" in length) is tuned like the top four strings of a guitar (DGBE).

Soprano   Concert   Tenor   Baritone

The Baritone Uke

The largest instrument in the ukulele family, the baritone is tuned DGBE with a lowered D, exactly like the first four strings of a guitar.

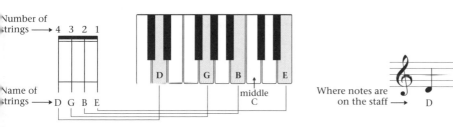

For guitar players the baritone uke is like a guitar without the top two strings. As a result, this makes the baritone uke particularly easy to play for guitarists. While an F chord on a soprano uke tuned GCEA is shaped differently on a baritone, the fingerings should all be familiar to a soprano player. For example, the F chord shape on a soprano becomes a C on a baritone. Here are some other examples:

GCEA shape:	B♭	B	C	D♭	D	E♭	E	F	G♭	G	A♭	A
is this on a DBGE uke:	F	F#	G	A♭	A	B♭	B	C	D♭	D	E♭	E

If you play baritone uke, you can still enjoy this book. You can either:

1) Play the chord names as written, but substitute bari chord fingerings. In this case, consult a good baritone uke chord book.

2) Play the fingerings as shown, but ignore the chord names and the written melody. This means that you will be playing and singing in a lower key.

SOMETHING

Words and Music by
GEORGE HARRISON

Some - thing in __ the way __ she moves, __
Some - thing in __ the smile __ she knows, __
Some - thing in __ the way __ she knows, __

__ at - tracts __ me like __ no oth - er love-
__ that I __ don't need __ no oth - er love-
__ and all __ I have __ to do is think

er.
er.
of her.

Some - thing in __ the way __ she woos
Some - thing in __ her style __ that shows
Some - thing in __ the things __ she shows __

_____ me. __
_____ me. __
_____ me. __

I don't want to leave __ her now, you

know I be - lieve __ and how. _____

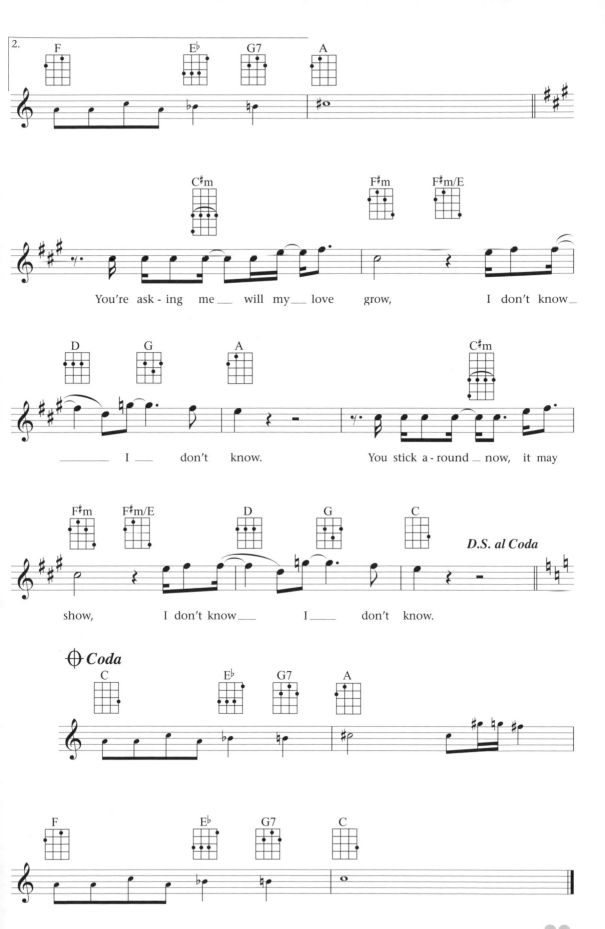

2.

You're ask-ing me ___ will my ___ love grow, I don't know ___

___ I ___ don't know. You stick a-round ___ now, it may

D.S. al Coda

show, I don't know ___ I ___ don't know.

⊕ **Coda**

SURFER GIRL

Words and Music by
BRIAN WILSON

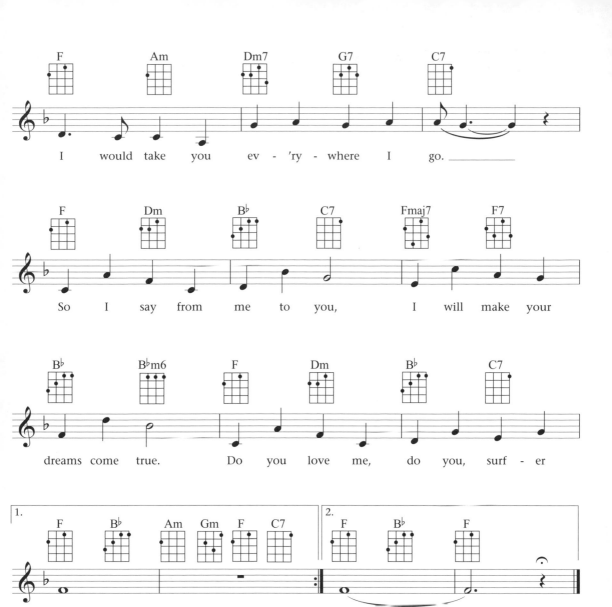

I would take you ev - 'ry - where I go. _____

So I say from me to you, I will make your

dreams come true. Do you love me, do you, surf - er

1.
girl?

2.
girl? _____

The Swagerty Surf-a-lele… perfect for the beach!

TIP-TOE THRU' THE TULIPS WITH ME

Lyric by
AL DUBIN

Music by
JOE BURKE

THOSE WERE THE DAYS

Words and Music by
GENE RASKIN

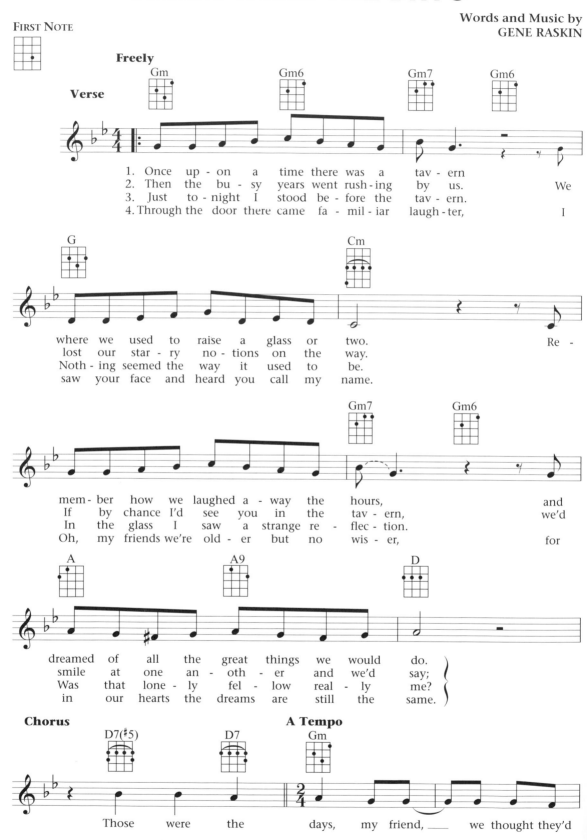

Verse

1. Once up-on a time there was a tav-ern
2. Then the bu-sy years went rush-ing by us. We
3. Just to-night I stood be-fore the tav-ern.
4. Through the door there came fa-mil-iar laugh-ter, I

where we used to raise a glass or two. Re-
lost our star-ry no-tions on the way.
Noth-ing seemed the way it used to be.
saw your face and heard you call my name.

mem-ber how we laughed a-way the hours, and
If by chance I'd see you in the tav-ern, we'd
In the glass I saw a strange re-flec-tion.
Oh, my friends we're old-er but no wis-er, for

dreamed of all the great things we would do.
smile at one an-oth-er and we'd say;
Was that lone-ly fel-low real-ly me?
in our hearts the dreams are still the same.

Chorus   **A Tempo**

Those were the days, my friend, ___ we thought they'd

nev - er end.___ We'd sing and dance for - ev - er and a

day. We'd live the life we chose,___ we'd fight and

nev - er lose,___ for we were young and sure___

___ to have our way. La la la la la la,___

___ la la la la la la,___ those were the days, oh

1.-3.

yes, those were the days.

4.

days. _____

UNDER THE BOARDWALK

Words and Music by
ARTIE RESNICK and KENNY YOUNG

Oh, when the 1. sun beats down __ and burns the
2. park you hear __ the hap - py

tar up - on the roof, __ and your
sound of a car - ou - sel, __ you can

shoes get so hot you wish your tired feet __ were fire -
al - most taste the hot - dogs and french - fries

- proof... Un - der the board - walk, __
they sell. Un - der the board - walk, __

down by the sea, __ yeah, on a
down by the sea, __ yeah, on a

blan - ket with my   ba - by's _____   where I'll _____ be. _____
blan - ket with my   ba - by's _____   where I'll _____ be. _____

(Un - der the board - walk)   Out   of   the sun _____ *(Un - der the*

board - walk)   we'll be   hav - in' some fun. _____ *(Un - der the*

board - walk)   Peo - ple   walk -in'   a -bove _____ *(Un - der the*

we'll be   fall - in'   in   love _____ un - der   the
board - walk) *(Un - der the*

board - walk,   board - walk.   From   the
board - walk,   board - walk.)   walk.

63

WHEN I'M SIXTY FOUR

Words and Music by
JOHN LENNON and PAUL McCARTNEY

FIRST NOTE

when I'm six-ty four?   Oo. _____

_____ You'll be old-er, too. _____

Ah, _____ and if you say the word, _____ I could

stay with you.   { I could be hand-y
                    { Send me a post-card,

mend-ing a fuse _____ when your lights have gone. _____
drop me a line _____ stat-ing point of view. _____

You can knit a sweat-er by the fire-side, _____
In-di-cate pre-cise-ly what you mean to say, _____

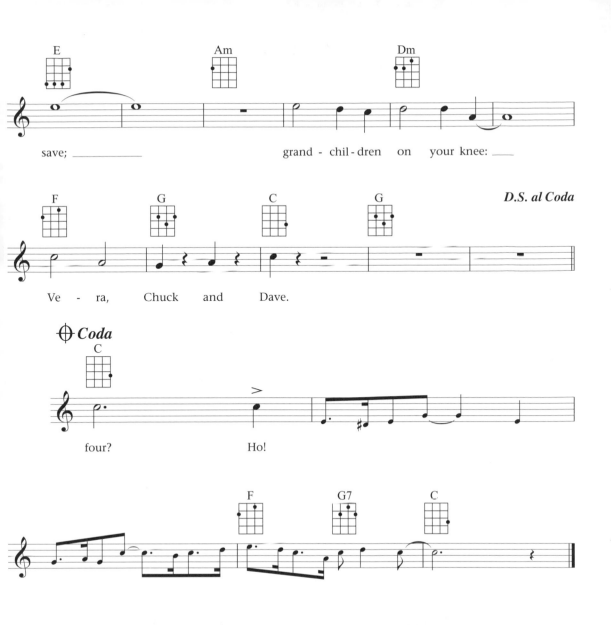

save; _____   grand - chil - dren   on   your knee: ___

D.S. al Coda

Ve - ra,   Chuck   and   Dave.

Coda

four?   Ho!

Never grow old! Jim and friends at Madame Tussaud's Wax Museum.

YELLOW SUBMARINE

Words and Music by
JOHN LENNON and PAUL McCARTNEY

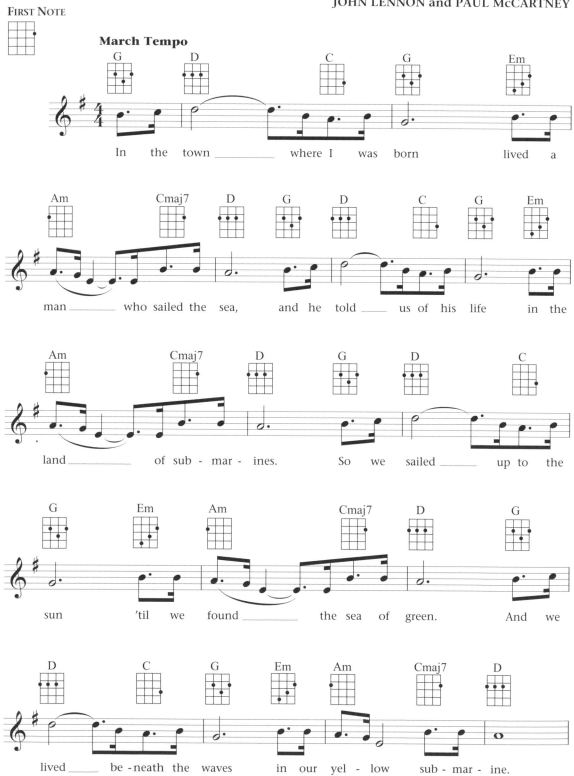

Chorus

We all live in a yel - low sub - mar - ine, yel - low sub - mar - ine,

yel - low sub - mar - ine. We all live in a yel - low sub - mar - ine,

yel - low sub - mar - ine, yel - low sub - mar - ine. {And our friends ___ are all on
As we live ___ a life of

board, man - y more of them live next door. And the
ease, ev - 'ry one of us has all we need: Sky of

band ___ be - gins to play:
blue ___ and sea of

D.S. and Fade

green in our yel - low sub - mar - ine.

69

WITH A LITTLE HELP FROM MY FRIENDS

Words and Music by
JOHN LENNON and PAUL McCARTNEY

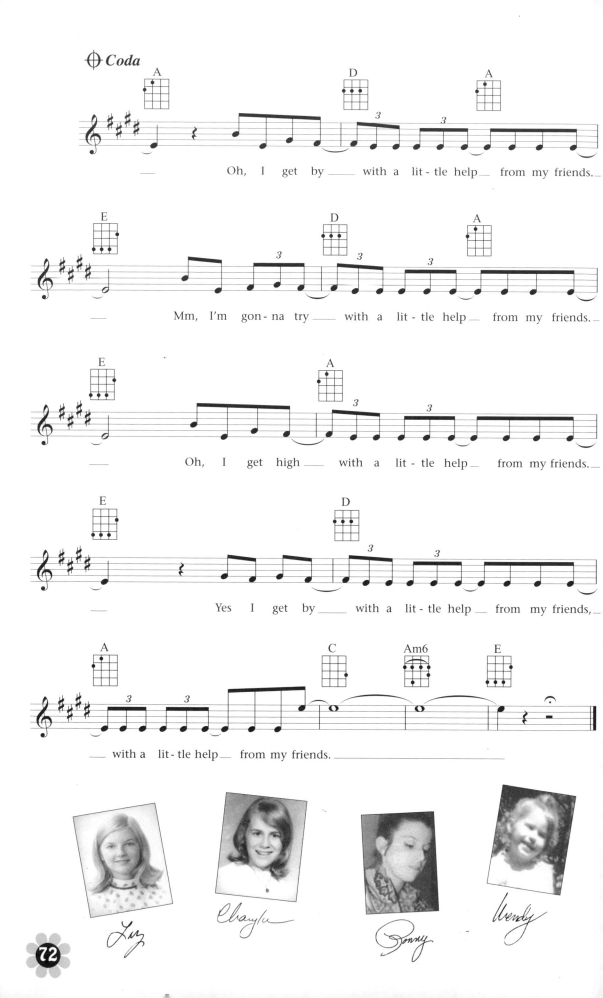

Coda

Oh, I get by ___ with a lit-tle help ___ from my friends. ___

Mm, I'm gon-na try ___ with a lit-tle help ___ from my friends. ___

Oh, I get high ___ with a lit-tle help ___ from my friends. ___

Yes I get by ___ with a lit-tle help ___ from my friends,

___ with a lit-tle help ___ from my friends. _____